John Adams

History Maker Bios

Jane Sutcliffe

LERNER PUBLICATIONS COMPANY • MINNEAPOLIS

Lerner Publications Company
A division of Lerner Publishing Group
241 First Avenue North
Minneapolis, MN 55401 U.S.A.

Website address: www.lernerbooks.com

Library of Congress Cataloging-in-Publication Data

Sutcliffe, Jane.
    John Adams / by Jane Sutcliffe.
        p.   cm. — (History maker bios)
    Includes bibliographical references and index.
    ISBN-13: 978–0–8225–5940–5 (lib. bdg. : alk. paper)
    ISBN-10: 0–8225–5940–4 (lib. bdg. : alk. paper)
    1. Adams, John, 1735–1826—Juvenile literature. 2. Presidents—United States—Biography—Juvenile literature. I. Title. II. Series.
    E322.S94 2006
    973.4'4092—dc22 [B]   2005032401

Manufactured in the United States of America
1 2 3 4 5 6 – JR – 11 10 09 08 07 06

TABLE OF CONTENTS

INTRODUCTION

Not many people can say that they helped invent a country. That's what John Adams did.

When he was born, the American colonies were part of Great Britain. John Adams helped change that. He helped free the colonies from British rule and create a new nation—the United States of America. He helped decide just what kind of country it was going to be. Then he spent most of his life serving the nation he had helped to create.

This is his story.

1 THE BRAINTREE FARM BOY

Where was young John Adams? That was easy. He was almost always outside, rambling about his father's farm.

John liked to make little boats and sail them on the ponds and brooks. He flew kites and skated and swam. Sometimes he hunted birds on the marsh—even when he was supposed to be in school.

John was born in October 1735. He grew up in the town of Braintree in the colony of Massachusetts. John's father wanted him to study hard and go to college. But John didn't like school. He didn't like his teacher. And he didn't like books. He told his father he wanted to be a farmer like him. (Farmers, he thought, didn't need school.)

JOHN ON THE GO

All his life, John was plump and round. But he was also strong, fit, and very active. He chopped wood, climbed cliffs, and took brisk walks through the woods and meadows of Braintree.

His father had other ideas. He saw that John was a bright boy. He found John a new teacher at a new school. John liked his new teacher. He began to study. By the time he was fifteen, he left the farm, kites, and hunting behind. He headed to Harvard College.

At Harvard, John found a new love—a love of books. This was a surprise! Not only did John like to read, he liked to talk too. With his talent for speaking, people said, he should be a lawyer.

Harvard College opened in 1636—more than one hundred years before John went to school there.

John graduated from Harvard. Then he taught at a small school like this one.

But first, John needed money. When he graduated in 1755, he took a teaching job. He taught school by day and studied law at night. At last, in 1758, he became a lawyer. He was twenty-three years old. He spent most of his money on books.

When John was twenty-five, his father died. He left John some land and a little farmhouse. John set up a law office there, with a special door for his clients. As business grew, the door opened more and more often.

John called young Abigail Smith (LEFT) Miss Adorable.

Of course, John wasn't always thinking about work. He had met smart, pretty Abigail Smith. John rode his horse to visit Abigail often. He called her Miss Adorable and wrote letters begging her for kisses. John was in love!

Abigail loved John too. In the fall of 1764, when John was twenty-eight and Abigail was nineteen, they were married. The very next year there was good news for the Adamses—and bad news for the colonies. The good news was a baby daughter named Abigail. Her parents called her Nabby.

The bad news was more taxes. The British king was using the taxes to get money from the colonies. First, there was a tax on printed paper. By the time John and Abigail's son John Quincy was born in 1767, that tax was gone. But there were new taxes on glass, paint, and tea.

The colonists didn't like the taxes one bit. In nearby Boston, angry people marched in the streets. They shouted, "Unfair!" and threw stones.

John was not a shouter. And he was certainly no stone thrower. Instead, he wrote articles speaking up for Americans' rights and liberties.

Colonists protest against British taxes.

John wrote that the colonists were not allowed to vote for the king's laws or leaders. So they shouldn't have to pay the king's tax, he said. He wanted the world to know "that we never can be slaves."

People liked John's spirited words. He met other men in Boston who wanted rights for the colonies. They called themselves patriots. They agreed to fight the taxes together.

John spent more and more time in Boston. He missed Abigail and the children. So in 1768, the whole family moved to Boston. John knew that a revolution had started in the minds and hearts of the American people. And he would be a part of it.

2 REVOLUTION

Liberty! Rights! Freedom! The British king was tired of the patriots' bold words. He sent his red-coated soldiers marching into Boston. He would show the people just who was in charge!

Still the people of Boston would not behave. They teased the soldiers and called them names. Where would it lead? On a cold, moonlit night in March 1770, everyone found out.

Colonial boys tease a British officer in Boston.

That night, shouting men and boys started throwing snowballs and oyster shells at British soldiers on King Street. The soldiers were frightened. They fired into the crowd. John heard the alarm bells calling the city to action. He thought that there must be a fire somewhere. He rushed into the street. But there was no fire. There was only blood on the snow where five American men had fallen.

The British soldiers and their captain were arrested for murder. And who would defend them in court? Why, John Adams! No other lawyer wanted the job. But John thought that everyone—even the hated redcoats—deserved a fair trial.

John's decision caused a few grumbles among his patriot friends. But mostly people respected what John was doing. He won his case too. The men were found not guilty of murder. The court decided they had fired in self-defense.

Paul Revere made this drawing of the shooting in Boston. The event became known as the Boston Massacre.

The Green Dragon Tavern in Boston was a popular place to eat, drink, and complain about the British.

John was busier than ever. Just a few months after the Boston Massacre, son Charles was born. (A daughter, Susanna, had died while still a baby). Baby Thomas was born two years later. By then, thirty-six-year-old John was a leader in the struggle against Great Britain.

There was still plenty to struggle against. The king had done away with most of the taxes. But he had kept the hated tax on tea. The people of Boston decided it was time to show the king what they thought of his taxes—and his tea.

One December night in 1773, some men dressed themselves up to look like Mohawk Indians. They sneaked aboard the ships that were carrying the tea. And they pitched every box of tea overboard.

John said the Boston Tea Party was "magnificent." But the king was furious. He shut down Boston's port. And he sent even more soldiers into the city.

Things were clearly getting worse. Leaders from other colonies were worried. They decided to hold a meeting to talk about what to do. It would be called the First Continental Congress.

Colonists cheered on the patriots as they threw British tea into Boston Harbor.

On August 10, 1774, John and three other men set out for the trip from Boston to Philadelphia. Crowds lined the streets to cheer for them. John should have been excited. Instead, he was filled with worry. Such a big job lay ahead!

John urged Congress to fight for the rights of all the colonies. Not everyone was eager to fight against Great Britain. Some thought the Massachusetts men were a bunch of hotheads. There were long arguments and longer speeches. Things went slowly.

BOOKS FOR ALL!

Once John asked his children what kind of present they'd like him to bring home from Philadelphia. Each child asked for a book. After all, they said, those were the only presents he ever gave anyway.

The First Continental Congress met in Carpenters' Hall in Philadelphia, Pennsylvania.

At last, the members agreed to stand by the Boston patriots. They demanded that the king put a stop to the unfair taxes. Then, in October, they went home.

Abigail and the children had moved back to Braintree. John was happy to see his family and his farm. But he was not ready to put down his pen. He kept writing.

Then, on the morning of April 19, 1775, British soldiers marched to the Massachusetts towns of Lexington and Concord. Armed Americans were waiting. Gunshots thundered in the morning mist. They were the first shots of war. The American Revolution had begun.

When John heard the news, he slapped a saddle on his horse. He rode to the battlefields to see for himself. Suddenly, he knew everything had changed. The struggle for liberty would no longer be fought with words. It would be fought with guns.

3 FREE AND INDEPENDENT STATES

Three weeks after the battles at Lexington and Concord, John was back in Philadelphia. He hated to leave Abigail and the children. But there was a war to fight and decisions to make. "In case of real danger," he wrote her, "fly to the woods with our children."

More than ever, John wanted the colonies to break away from Great Britain. Still, some members of Congress disagreed.

John thought the Continental Congress talked too much and did not pay attention to the war in Massachusetts.

While the members argued ("nibbling and quibbling," John called it once), a war was going on in Massachusetts. Abigail's letters to John told it all. British soldiers had control of Boston. Nearby towns were in a panic.

Did Congress know what was happening? she asked John. "Can they realize what we suffer?"

"They can't. They don't," John replied. But *he* did. He had to do something to help the American soldiers fighting in Massachusetts. They needed training and supplies. They needed a commander.

On June 14, 1775, John asked Congress to give George Washington the job. Washington was a tall, brave soldier from Virginia. He would lead the new American army. This was no small task, and John knew it. "The liberties of America depend upon him," he said.

There was more work to do. John made a list. The colonies had to print money. They had to start taxing people to pay for the war. They had to draw up agreements with other countries.

GOOD MORNING, JOHN
Creating a new nation was a big job. John got up before dawn and was hard at work at seven in the morning. He didn't stop until eleven at night.

John was full of plans for the new nation.

John was already thinking of the colonies as a new, free nation. He had even thought out how the new government would work. All the power should be split up, he said. That way, each part would check and balance the others.

Now he just had to show the slowpokes in Congress that the time for independence had come. Little by little, they began to see things John's way. At last, they agreed to a vote. They would decide whether to break with Great Britain once and for all.

If the congressmen did vote for independence, they'd need to tell the world. They'd have to explain why they were right in declaring their freedom. They needed a Declaration of Independence. John would help find the words for that declaration.

John's friend Thomas Jefferson did the actual writing. ("You can write ten times better than I can," John told him.) John just made a few changes. When it was done, it was a powerful statement of the rights of all people. "We hold these truths to be self-evident, that all men are created equal . . ."

John (SECOND FROM RIGHT) helped to write the Declaration of Independence.

John urged the Contintental Congresss to accept the Declaration of Independence.

The day for the vote arrived. But first, John decided to say a few words. He hadn't really prepared a speech. He had no notes. But he poured all his love for his country into what he said. He spoke for two hours. His powerful words, Jefferson said, "moved us from our seats."

On July 2, 1776, Congress voted to make the colonies "free and independent states." Two days later, on July 4, they voted to accept the Declaration of Independence. The ties to Great Britain were cut forever. The United States of America was born.

Of course, the king didn't care about the Americans' declaration. These were *his* colonies! So the war went on.

In November 1777, John finally went home to the farm and his family. He was forty-two years old. Except for short visits, he'd been away for four years. But he finally told Abigail that he was home to stay. He looked forward to being a family man and a lawyer again. He felt he had done all he could for his country.

4 TRAVELS WITH JOHN

John had been home only three weeks when he heard the news. The Continental Congress was sending him to France! His job was to ask the French government for help in fighting the war.

John thought of all sorts of reasons not to go. Crossing the ocean would be dangerous. He would miss Abigail and the children terribly. And he didn't even speak French!

But his country needed him again. That settled the matter.

On a windy winter day in 1778, John stepped aboard the ship that would take him across the ocean. Ten-year-old John Quincy went too. The voyage was horrible. Crashing storms tore the ship's sails to rags. A British ship attacked them. John was nearly hit by a cannonball!

At last, they arrived safely—only to find that John's job was already done. The French had decided to send money and guns for the war. All that was left to do was clean up some messy paperwork. In spring 1779, father and son sailed home again.

Young John Quincy Adams

John spent a lot of time thinking and writing his ideas about government.

John had never stopped thinking about how government should work. At home, he started writing a plan for the state of Massachusetts. He put in all of his ideas about checks and balances. He wrote that government should be split into different parts called branches. Each one should have a role and a say in how things were done. In time, John's ideas became the law of the state.

But Congress wasn't done with John Adams. One month after John finished the Massachusetts Constitution, Congress sent him back to Europe. Both John Quincy and Charles went with him this time.

John was busier than ever. He represented his country in Holland. He helped work out a peace treaty with Great Britain. When that was signed in September 1783, the American Revolution was over. The colonists had won, and the United States of America was an independent nation.

In the 1700s, Amsterdam, Holland, was an important center for world trade. About 200,000 people lived there.

John was proud of all he had done for his country. But he was not happy. He missed Abigail. They had been apart for most of nine years! "I would give the world to be with you tomorrow," he wrote her. Still, Congress wanted him to stay in Europe.

So instead of waiting for John to come home, Abigail joined him and John Quincy in Europe. Nabby went too. (Charles had gone back home.) John was delighted to have Abigail with him at last.

American artist Mather Brown met Nabby in Europe. He painted this picture of her.

Thomas Jefferson was in Paris when John Adams and his family arrived.

He still had work to do in Paris, France. So the family moved into a grand house near the city. John's old friend Thomas Jefferson was in Paris too. He and John became even closer. Jefferson often joined the family for dinner or to see the sights of the city.

One day, John received exciting news. He would be the first American to represent the new nation in Great Britain. He would meet the British king face-to-face.

On June 1, 1785, John stood before King George III. His voice trembled with feeling. He told the king he spoke for "the United States of America." How proud he must have been to say those words! He said he hoped there would once again be ties of friendship between the two countries.

In the spring of 1788, John and his family went home at last. As they sailed into Boston Harbor, they were surprised and delighted! Cheering crowds lined the docks. Cannons boomed and church bells rang, all to welcome John Adams home.

5 PRESIDENT ADAMS

T he United States of America had a
new set of laws and rules of
government. It was called the U.S.
Constitution. It was very much like the
constitution John had written for his home
state. John was not there when the country's
constitution was written. But his ideas were.

The new laws called for an election.
Everyone expected George Washington to
be chosen president—and he was. And
fifty-three-year-old John Adams became
vice president.

John was ready to jump right into his new job. But there wasn't much to do. The vice president was there mostly in case the president died. John said he had the most unimportant job ever invented!

Of course, he couldn't help giving an opinion or two. Once he suggested that the president be called His Highness, the President. He thought that showed respect. But most people laughed.

Others didn't think his suggestion was so funny. They thought John wanted to go back to having a king. This was a serious charge! Even old friend Thomas Jefferson thought some of John's ideas were crazy—and said so. Their warm friendship turned cool.

HOW DARE HE!

John always told people exactly what he thought. Sometimes, though, he hurt people's feelings. They felt he was being rude and thoughtless. That didn't make him very popular!

George Washington was the president of the United States from 1789 to 1797.

By 1796, George Washington wanted a rest. Two men hoped to take his place as president—John Adams and Thomas Jefferson. John won by three votes. Jefferson came in second. According to the laws at the time, that made him vice president. But these two had very different opinions. How would this work?

President Adams had no time to worry. He was trying to prevent a war with France. The French had helped Americans win independence. But times had changed. French ships were attacking U.S. ships.

Americans urged the president to declare war. John wanted to be ready. He created a new Navy Department. He added soldiers to the army. But he would not declare war. Later, on his own, he sent new representatives to France to work for peace. He didn't even ask Congress for permission.

In the 1790s, France was a much larger and more powerful country than the United States. John Adams did not want war with France.

John Adams signed some unpopular laws while he was president.

John Adams

Some people worried that French people in the United States might be spies. Congress passed laws limiting the rights of people from other countries. The laws also made it a crime to write articles criticizing the government. The laws were not John's idea. But he supported them. He thought they were needed in case of war.

Other people, including Thomas Jefferson, were shocked. They said that the laws were against the U.S. Constitution. The new laws were the worst mistake of John's presidency. He wasn't turning out to be a popular president.

In 1800, John was sixty-four years old and tired. A new presidential election was coming. But first, John and Abigail had to move. A grand new house was waiting for them in the new capital city of Washington. Someday the house would be known as the White House. So far, it was still empty and half-finished. The Adamses lit the fires to stay warm in the cold, damp house and wondered how long they'd be staying.

The new Washington home of the U.S. president had more than one hundred rooms.

In December, they found out. John had lost the election. Thomas Jefferson would be the new president. The only good news was that a peace agreement had been signed with France. John had kept the country out of war. But the news came too late to help him.

John and Abigail went back to their farm. At last, John was free to be a farmer, just as he'd wanted to be as a boy. He built stone walls and worried about hay and called himself Farmer John.

John and Abigail needed a home with lots of room for visiting children and grandchildren.

Abigail was married to John for fifty-four years.

John and Abigail grew old together. In 1818, John said good-bye to Abigail for the last time. She died at the age of seventy-three.

Lonely and sad, John surrounded himself with books. He wrote letters to old friends. One New Year's Day, John took a deep breath and picked up his pen. He wrote to Thomas Jefferson. Jefferson wrote back. They set aside their hurt feelings. "While I breathe I shall be your friend," John told him.

In March 1825, John was proud when John Quincy became the sixth president of the United States. But he was too weak to attend any of the celebrations. On the Fourth of July 1826—the country's fiftieth birthday—John died. Before taking his last breath, he whispered, "Thomas Jefferson survives." He was wrong. His friend had died a few hours earlier. The two heroes of the fight for freedom had left the stage together.

TIMELINE

In the year . . .

1755   John graduated from Harvard College.

1758   he became a lawyer.

1764   he married Abigail Smith.   Age 28

1765   his daughter Nabby was born.

1767   his son John Quincy was born.

1770   the Boston Massacre took place in March.
       John's son Charles was born in May.

1772   John's son Thomas was born.

1773   the Boston Tea Party took place.

1774   John attended the Continental Congress.

1775   the Revolutionary War began.

1776   he helped Thomas Jefferson prepare the
       Declaration of Independence.
       Congress approved the Declaration on July 4.   Age 40

1778   John became a representative in France.

1779   he wrote the Massachusetts constitution.

1785   he became the first U.S. representative to
       Great Britain.

1789   he became the first vice president of the
       United States.

1797   he became the second president of the   Age 61
       United States.

1800   he became the first president to live in the
       White House.

1818   Abigail died.

1825   his son John Quincy became the sixth
       president of the United States.

1826   John died on July 4.   Age 90

INDEPENDENCE FOREVER

John thought the United States would celebrate its birthday on July 2. That's the date the American colonies voted for independence. "The second day of July 1776 will be the most memorable . . . in the history of America," he said.

Instead, we celebrate on the Fourth of July—the date that the Declaration of Independence was passed. But whatever the date, John knew that Independence Day was the most important date in the country's history. He told Abigail that future Americans would celebrate the day "with pomp and parade, with shows, games, sports, guns, bells, bonfires, and illuminations from one end of this continent to the other from this time forward forever more."

And so we do.

In New York City, fireworks light up the Statue of Liberty on July 4, 1886.

FURTHER READING

Fradin, Dennis Brindell. *The Signers: The Fifty-Six Stories Behind the Declaration of Independence.* New York: Walker & Company, 2002. Learn more about John Adams and the other people who signed the Declaration of Independence.

Gherman, Beverly. *First Son and President: A Story about John Quincy Adams.* Minneapolis: Millbrook Press, 2006. Find out more about the life of John and Abigail's eldest son, who became the sixth U.S. president.

Harness, Cheryl. *The Revolutionary John Adams.* Washington, DC: National Geographic, 2003. Learn more about how John Adams was a unique and important U.S. leader.

Meisner, James Jr., and Amy Ruth. *American Revolutionaries and Founders of the Nation.* Berkeley Heights, NJ: Enslow Publishers, 1999. Explore the exciting stories of early American patriots.

Sherrow, Victoria. *Thomas Jefferson.* Minneapolis: Lerner Publications Company, 2003. Read about John's vice president and good friend.

St. George, Judith. *John and Abigail Adams: An American Love Story.* New York: Holiday House, 2001. Find out more about John and Abigail's relationship.

Sutcliffe, Jane. *Abigail Adams.* Minneapolis: Lerner Publications Company, 2006. Read more about John Adams' First Lady, who had many strong ideas of her own.

Wagner, Heather Lehr. *Great American Presidents: John Adams.* Philadelphia: Chelsea House Publishers, 2004. Take another look at the second U.S. president.

WEBSITES

Biography of John Adams
http://www.whitehouse.gov/history/presidents/ja2.html
Visit this website for John's official White House biography.

National Archives Experience—The Declaration of Independence
http://www.archives.gov/national-archives-experience/
charters/declaration_join_the_signers.html
Learn more about the Declaration of Independence at this site.

SELECT BIBLIOGRAPHY

Adams, John. "A Dissertation on the Canon and Feudal Law." *TeachingAmericanHistory.org*. N.d. http://teachingamericanhistory.org/library/index.asp?documentprint=43 (December 19, 2005).

Butterfield, L. H., ed. *Diary and Autobiography of John Adams*. 4 vols. Cambridge, MA: The Belknap Press of Harvard University Press, 1961.

Butterfield, L. H., M. Friedlander, and M. J. Kline, eds. *The Book of Abigail and John: Selected Letters of the Adams Family, 1762–1784*. Cambridge, MA: Harvard University Press, 1975.

McCullough, David. *John Adams*. New York: Simon & Schuster, 2001.

Shuffleton, Frank, ed. *The Letters of John and Abigail Adams*. New York: Penguin Books, 2004.

Withey, Lynne. *Dearest Friend: A Life of Abigail Adams*. New York: Simon & Schuster, 1981.

INDEX

Acknowledgments

For photographs and artwork: Library of Congress, pp. 4 (LC-USZ62-13002), 8 (LC-USZ62-96223), 11 (LC-USZ61-536), 15 (LC-USZC4-4600), 17 (LC-USZC4-523), 22 (LC-USZ62-45328), 37 (LC-USZC4-2968), 39 (LC- USZ62-67440), 40 (LC-USZ62-3068), 45 (LC-USZ62-85642); © North Wind Picture Archives, pp. 9, 10, 14, 30; American Antiquarian Society, p. 16; © Peter Harholdt/CORBIS, p. 23; National Archives, pp. 24, 25; Peter Newark's American Pictures, p. 26; Adams National Historical Park, pp. 29, 32, 41; The Art Archive/Bibliotheque des Arts Decoratifs Paris/Dagli Orti, p. 31; Independence National Historical Park, p. 33; The Art Archive/Musee Carnavalet Paris/Dagli Orti, p. 38; Society for the Preservation of New England Antiquities, p. 42. Front Cover: National Archives. Back Cover: Adams National Historical Park.

For quoted material: p. 12, John Adams, "Instructions of the Town of Braintree to Their Representative, 1765." *American Passages,* n.d., http://www.wadsworth.com/history_d/special_features/ext/ap/chapter5/5.1.braintree.html (December 19, 2005); pp. 17, 22, 45, L. H. Butterfield, ed.,. *Diary and Autobiography of John Adams, vol. 1–4* (Cambridge, MA, The Belknap Press of Harvard University Press, 1961); pp. 21, 22, 23, 32, 45, L. H. Butterfield, M. Friedlander, and M. J. Kline, ed., *The Book of Abigail and John: Selected Letters of the Adams Family, 1762-1784* (Cambridge, MA: Harvard University Press, 1975); p. 22, Frank Shuffleton, ed., *The Letters of John and Abigail Adams* (New York: Penguin Books, 2004); pp. 25, 26, 42, 43, David McCullough, *John Adams* (New York: Simon & Schuster, 2001); p. 25, "Declaration of Independence," *The National Archives Experience,* n.d., http://www.archives.gov/national-archives-experience/charters/declaration_transcript.html (March 22, 2006).